Ghosts

Kathy Galashan

Published in association with The Basic Skills Agency

Hodder & Stoughton

A MEMB'   JOSEPH PRIESTLEY COLLEGE   ʻ GROUP

23254

Acknowledgements
Cover: Derek Stafford/Fortean Picture

Photos: p 3 © Marina Jackson/Fortean Picture Library; p 18 © Harry Lester Andrews/Fortean Picture Library; p 24 © Adam Hart-Davis/Fortean Picture Library; p 26 © Tony O'Rahilly/Fortean Picture Library

Illustrations: Maureen Carter

Every effort has been made to trace copyright holders of material reproduced in this book. Any rights not acknowledged will be acknowledged in subsequent printings if notice is given to the publisher.

Orders; please contact Bookpoint Ltd, 39 Milton Park, Abingdon, Oxon OX14 4TD. Telephone (44) 01235 400414, Fax: (44) 01235 400454. Lines are open from 9.00–6.00, Monday to Saturday, with a 24 hour message answering service. Email address: orders@bookpoint.co.uk

British Library Cataloguing in Publication Data
A catalogue record for this title is available from the British Library

ISBN 0 340 80072 0

First published 2001
Impression number   10 9 8 7 6 5 4 3 2 1
Year   2007 2206 2005 2004 2003 2002 2001

Typeset by SX Composing DTP, Rayleigh, Essex.
Printed in Great Britain for Hodder & Stoughton Educational, a division of Hodder Headline Plc, 338 Euston Road, London NW1 3BH by Redwood Books Ltd, Trowbridge, Wiltshire.

Contents

1   What is a Ghost?

What is a ghost?
A headless man in strange clothes.
A woman that walks through walls.
A shape that appears and disappears
in front of your eyes.

A dead person that walks and moves.
A cold feeling that send shivers
down your back.
Strange noises.
Objects flying round a room.

People see ghosts at night and in the day.
Ghosts appear in buildings, old and new.
They appear in ships and aeroplanes.
They are in the open
and in dark corners.
There are ghosts of the living and the dead.

People know that strange things
really do happen.
This book tells ghost stories.
It gives possible explanations
for these stories.
It looks at ideas
which try to explain ghosts.

Do ghosts exist?
Nobody knows the answer.
What do you think?
Ask around.
It is surprising how many people
have seen a ghost.

This little boy may be looking at the ghost of his great-grandmother.

2   The Haunted Jet

This is a story of a haunted jet plane.
Is it true?
Many people believe it is.

In 1972, Flight 401
set off from New York
in a L1011 jet.
The pilot was Captain Bob Loft.
The engineer was Don Repo.
There were 176 people on board.

As the plane flew over swampland
in Florida it lost height.
The pilot saw the swampland
ahead of them.
Too late.
It was too late to climb,
to get higher.

The plane crashed.
The plane came down
in the middle of the night.
It crashed into icy water and long grass.
The rescue was very difficult.
Only 77 people survived.
Both the captain and the engineer
died that night.

Three months after the crash,
people began to see and hear
strange things on L1101 planes.
A woman sat next to a man in a pilot's uniform.
He looked very pale.
The woman called over a stewardess
and the man disappeared.
The woman went crazy.
She screamed and screamed.

After the flight,
she looked at pictures of all the staff
who worked for the airline.
She picked out Don Repo,
the engineer of Flight 401.

One woman thought she had seen the ghost of Don Repo.

Another time a voice came over the speakers.
'Fasten your seatbelts.'
It was not the voice of any crew member
but it was over the place
where Flight 401 crashed.

Yet another time,
an engineer went to check the plane.
It was flying to New York.
He found Don Repo in the engineer's seat.
The ghost said,
'There will never be another crash on L1101.
We will not let it happen.'

A man called John Fuller wrote a book
about the Ghost of Flight 401.
When he started,
he didn't believe in ghosts.
He talked to many people.
The more people he talked to
the more he believed in ghosts.
He couldn't explain all the things
they told him.

3   Haunted Places

Berry Pomeroy Castle, Devon

Berry Pomeroy Castle has been empty
for over two hundred years.
Many strange things have been reported.

A man was exploring with a friend.
He felt a tight band round his head.
He saw a dim blue light
moving across a high wall.
He was terrified.

Another time, a couple
were walking their dog.
Suddenly, the air became
freezing cold.
The dog howled.
It's hair stood on end
and it ran away
as fast as it could.

A woman was on a walk
with her two children.
She needed a key to a locked gate.
There was an old man
and she told the children to ask for a key.
They could not see anyone.
She went over herself
but the man looked strange
and she felt frightened.
She did not dare go near him.
The children saw nothing.

Many people tell of strange noises.
They have heard doors banging,
the sound of horses,
and a baby crying.

Some people reported
going back in time.

Mr Hills and his family
went on a helicopter ride.
They saw castle walls and a roof
where today there are ruins.
They saw smoke coming from the chimneys.
They went back to the castle on foot.
There was no roof.
It was covered in scaffolding.
They had seen no scaffolding from the air.
They had seen the castle
as it used to be.

These are just a few of the stories
from the castle.

Norway 1960

Two young scientists were camping
in the north of Norway.
They camped in the wilderness
many many miles from roads, shops and houses.

From the first night
many strange things started to happen.
A pan of porridge was left in a hole near the water.
There was a large rock on top.
The next morning, the porridge was gone
but the rock was still in the same place.
How could an animal put the rock back?

In the middle of the night
they heard the noise of trucks and jeeps.
The noise came nearer and nearer.
It stopped just in front of the tents.
The noise went on for a long time.

The next night they heard screams and cries.
They heard the cries of men, women and children.
They were terrified.
The hair stood up
on the back of their necks.
The cries went on for over an hour.
There was no sleep that night.

They went back to the village
at the end of their trip
and told the local people their story.

The villagers had a story too.
There used to be a village by the lake
where they had camped.
Then in World War II
the Germans occupied Norway.
One night in 1942
the Germans had passed that place
on their way north.
Everyone in the village had been killed.

4 Explanations

How can these
and hundreds of other stories be true?
How can people see, hear and feel things
that are not there?

Maybe the men in Norway
had read about the war
but forgotten the story.
Maybe they heard sounds
from a long way away.
Sound can travel far on a quiet night.
They heard sounds
and put them into a dream.
But how did two people
have the same dream
at the same time?

And what about the porridge
that went missing?
Was it an animal?
Maybe the young men didn't look
carefully enough
Maybe they didn't see the signs.

The villagers in Norway were Sami people.
They believe that spirits
travel on old roads and tracks.
When the way is blocked or disturbed
the spirits are restless.
Then they cross into the world of today.

We all want to understand
the world we live in.
There are some general ideas or theories
people use to explain ghosts.
Decide for yourself
if they could be true.

5 The Energy Theory

It may be that people
and all living things give off energy.
Somehow and in some way
that energy can be picked up later.

Perhaps when terrible things happen
the energy is stronger
and leaves a trace, or a mark.
Perhaps some people pick up the energy
more easily than others.

Some people believe an energy trace
is a bit like a camera film.
With a camera you take a picture
but you can only see it
when the film is developed.

Maybe the same is true of an energy trace.
The energy is locked in a place.
People see it when the time is right.

What is energy?
That is a question that is hard to answer.

This photo shows a possible ghost from a nearby grave.

6   Levels of Consciousness

Another theory looks at
how the human brain works.
The brain is always working
but not always in the same way.

It is possible to read brain activity
with an EEG machine.
This machine reads brain waves.
It shows that the brain waves are different
when we are awake or asleep,
busy or relaxed.
The brain shows a special pattern
for dreaming sleep.
In a dream we see, hear and feel
all sorts of things.

Maybe people who see ghosts
are really dreaming.
Their brain is working in an unusual way.
They are awake
but the brain is in a dream state.

7 Real Life Explanations

Perhaps there are different answers
for different stories.
Some stories have real life answers.

Vic Tandy was a scientist.
He worked in a lab.
Strange things happened.
He sweated but the lab was cold.
His hands shook.

He saw a moving shape
out of the corner of his eye.

He took his dog into the lab.
It howled when it came into the room.

People said the lab was haunted.
He was a scientist.
He didn't believe in ghosts.
He tried to find out the reason.

It was an electric fan.
When he took the fan away
the strange things stopped.
The fan gave out a very low sound wave.
The sound was too low
for people to hear
but dogs could hear it.

8   Ghost Hunting

There are professional ghost hunters,
people who earn money
checking out ghost stories.
Is it a fake?
Is there a real life explanation?

Ghost hunters talk to
all the people involved.
If they think there is a ghost
they will try to see or hear it.
Maybe a room is haunted.
Ghost hunters seal off the room.
They have to make sure that
no one is playing tricks.

They may tie cotton across doors and windows.
They may sprinkle flour
on stairs or the floor.
This will make it harder
for someone to trick them.

They set up equipment.
They measure temperature and vibrations.
They make a plan of the room
so they will know if anything is moved.
They have tape recorders
to record sounds
and cameras to take pictures.

Some ghost hunters believe
that animals can see or feel ghosts.
They take cats or dogs with them.
If there is a ghost
the animals behave strangely.

Ghost hunters find
that many stories can be explained.
Some are fakes.
Some are a trick of the light
or a result of the weather.
But many can't be explained.
Ghost hunters hear about
events that have no explanation.

These ghost hunters are testing to see whether the shakes in
this building are due to ghosts or water underground.

9 Photographs of Ghosts

In 1995, there was a fire
at Wem town hall.
Photographs were taken.
One showed a girl
on the burning staircase.

In 1677, a young girl
burned down a house.
Her candle set fire to the roof.
The house was on the same land
as the town hall.

Maybe the photograph was
a trick of light and shadow.
Maybe it was a double exposure.
This means two photos
were taken on the same frame.
Maybe there really was a ghost.

The photograph of a girl on the burning staircase at
Wem Town Hall.

There are many photos of ghosts.
Some are fakes.
Sometimes experts cannot explain
the photos away.
They cannot say how they are faked
or explain the trick.

Are there ghosts?
Nobody knows.
There are many things
we don't understand.

Do we understand enough
about how we see the world?
Do we understand what happens
after death?

We do know that
we don't know all the answers.
There are many mysteries
that are not explained.

GLOSSARY

haunted   A place where ghosts are seen and strange things happen

a theory   an explanation

a mystery   something that cannot be explained

consciousness   how aware a person is of what is happening around them

EEG machine   a machine that reads brain waves

vibrations   shaking movements

a fake   something that pretends to be what it isn't

double exposure   two photo images on the same picture

professional   someone who gets paid

scaffolding   boards put up by builders. It lets you work off the ground